To

Robert H. Trisco

as a souvenir of our pleasant
meeting in London in
July, 1956.

John Tracy Ellis

October 1, 1956

American Catholics
and the Intellectual Life

AMERICAN CATHOLICS

and the

INTELLECTUAL LIFE

By

JOHN TRACY ELLIS

THE HERITAGE FOUNDATION, INC.
75 East Wacker Drive
Chicago 1, Illinois

Permission to reprint this article
from *THOUGHT* is gratefully acknowledged.

Prefatory Note

This study by Monsignor Ellis is making an unusually important contribution to the interpretation and, perhaps, even the direction of our times on the relationship of Catholicism to American intellectual life.

This particular paper is the most provocative, quite possibly the best, of many which have appeared in recent months as the "great debate" on Catholic American intellectualism has developed. That debate entered its present phase with the publication of Monsignor Ellis' address in St. Louis on May 14, 1955. This address defined, for the present at least, the *status quaestionis* to which all serious discussion of the matter must address itself until the issues raised in it have been faced and settled.

Monsignor Ellis' paper provoked a reaction that is in itself irrefutable evidence of how well timed and accurate are his contentions. A great number of others were emboldened by his statements to lift their own voices on the urgency of a re-evaluation of Catholic intellectual life in the United States, and their witness frequently added proof both that the cause is critical and that it is far from hopeless. The passion with which the few dissenters from Monsignor Ellis' position set forth their indignant reservations proved that he had touched a tender nerve. In an article in AMERICA for April 7, Monsignor Ellis himself summarized some of the reactions to his original piece. He has received several hundred letters. All but four seem to be in agreement with his analysis.

The article itself is an important contribution to the documentation on the "great debate," but there is no reason to believe that all the reactions are by any means yet registered. One awaits with mingled sentiments of dread and curiosity this season's commencement addresses, for example!

What we have called the "great debate" raging here in the United States at the moment is doubtless no more than a phase within our own land of an argument that has been going on in Europe for decades. Traditionally, the European intellectual has been acknowledged by his contemporaries, even those who might disagree with him, to have a "vocation" beyond the limits of his own profession of writing or science or teaching. It is a vocation quite apart from that of the functionary or representative of Church or of State, and it has obvious and grave perils as well as elements of prestige. These perils are as real as ignominy, exile or prison, even death, the frequent destinies of the traditional intellectuals in Europe. And yet, the intellectual has usually enjoyed a veneration in Europe which scarcely has a parallel in the common American attitude towards those who take on the valiant role of questioner, critic or intellectual trail blazer. The reader will note the "witty extravagance" which Monsignor Ellis recalls as differentiating the attitudes of Europeans and Americans towards intellectuals: in the Old World an ordinary mortal on seeing a professor tipped his hat, while in America he taps his head.

Such a suspicious attitude toward the intellectual life is far from being an exclusively Catholic phenomenon in the United States. Indeed, this kink in the American character generally may be due, as an editorial in the *Washington Post and Times Herald* pointed out on December 19, 1955, to specifically non-Catholic sociological and even theological influences on the formation of our national character. For example, the thoroughly practical problems confronting the first settlers on New England's stern and rock-bound coast no doubt intensified the predisposition of their Calvinist theology to emphasize results rather than theories and to reverence achievement rather than abstract speculation. There is a characteristically American esteem for the word "industry," in all its senses, which has never been accorded to the word "intellectual" or any of its variations.

The anti-intellectual attitude, however, is more unbecoming and embarrassing in Catholics because it is so entirely inconsistent with any authentic Catholic position. So many of the heresies which have wounded the Church and despoiled her of whole nations have been voluntarist heresies, anti-intellectual in their roots and pretensions, that it is bitterly ironic when anti-intellectualism threatens to become characteristic of those who have remained faithful to her obedience.

One wonders whether Catholics themselves always appreciate the extent to which the battles of the Church against the modern heresies have been at one and the same time battles against the heresy of anti-intellectualism. Luther's "stat pro ratione voluntas," his voluntaristic *fides fiducialis* with its repudiation of the intellectual elements in the act of faith, and his violent but typical description of the intellect as the "devil's whore," are as much the evidence of his departure from Catholic traditions as any of his theses nailed to the chapel door. The blind fatalism of Calvin, the perverse austerities of Jansenism, the sentimentality and exaltation of instinct or religious emotion which, for all its show of scholarship, characterized Modernism, are all typical of the heresies which have divided the Christian flock in these last four centuries. In defending supernatural revelation against these the Church was at the same time defending the validity of natural reason and the primacy of the intellect over the will, the emotions, the instincts or any of the other faculties to which voluntarism has always appealed, whether in Luther's dogma, the moral theories of Jansenius, the religious psychology of the moderns or the political philosophy of totalitarianism.

We usually think of the Council of Trent, the Vatican Council and the Syllabus against Modernism in terms of the defense of revealed dogmas, and such, of course, they were. But he understands them poorly who fails to perceive that they were frequently Catholic affirmations of the validity of reason as well as of the reality of revelation, and that they bore witness to the essential part of rational elements even in the supernatural act of faith, and to the divine origin of the primacy and rights of the intellect in the natural order.

It is, therefore, a problem for the Church when any who might be taken as her representatives in any sense in the world of the campus, the press, or the forum reveal contempt for that "wild, living intellect of man" of which Cardinal Newman spoke, or cynicism about the slow, sometimes faltering, but patient, persevering processes by which the intellectual seeks to wrest some measure of order from the chaos about us.

The problem is manifold: Monsignor Ellis' paper and others which followed give good hope that its solution may be in process of realization. First of all, there is a problem of definitions. What precisely do we now mean when we use the word intellectual and when we speak of either the virtues or faults of "intellectualism"? It is this initial problem which has been highlighted by the editor of the Brooklyn *Tablet* in his evaluation of recent writings on the subject.

Then there is a problem which we can best call spiritual or apostolic. What is the vocation of the intellectual in the life of the Church? How can he best bear his specifically intellectual witness, a witness which may involve a living martyrdom, given the temper of the times and the suspicion with which even his own will all too often views his gifts and his works? How shall we persuade intellectuals to find in Christ, the *Logos,* the Eternal Word made flesh to dwell among us, a divine prototype of their special vocation and unique dignity, as we have persuaded workers to find their model in the Carpenter's Son, Christian youth to find a model in the youthful Christ's obedience to Joseph and Mary at Nazareth, and patriotic citizens to see the exemplar of their proper loyalty in the Christ who paid the coin of tribute and wept tears of predilection over the capital city of his nation? A spirituality of Christian humanism, centered about the concept of Christ the Divine Intellectual, is a critical need of our generation if the evidence presented here proves as much as we have good reason to believe it does.

The problem of the apostolic role of the Catholic intellectual cannot be too often emphasized. Father Raymond L. Bruckberger, O.P., our friendly French critic, in an article in *Harper's Magazine* for February 1956 on the patriotic responsibilities of the American intellectual, makes a point worthy of meditation by Catholic intellectuals who sincerely seek to understand their contemporary religious responsibilities. The American intellectual often tends to say that his country has failed him, that she will not give him the honor which is his due, and that he feels like a spiritual exile. Perhaps, the contrary is more nearly true, and the American intellectual is more deeply missed than is at first apparent. When the intellectual turns his back on his country and confines himself to berating her, his place remains empty, all the while that he complains that he has no place at all. A more valiant generation of European intellectuals accepted it as their destiny to be unappreciated and mocked for false prophets; in this they found a secret consolation and often their abiding glory.

Catholic intellectuals have a point for meditation here. Intellectually gifted Catholics suffer all too often from a "whining" tendency in their attitude toward the Church. They lament that they are not sufficiently appreciated or encouraged. They berate the indifference of their fellow Catholics to their vocation. In a curious paradox on the lips of Christians, particularly Christians with presumably keener powers of insight and understanding than the rest, they protest against being made martyrs. Where in the New Testament, the Church of the Fathers, or the history of the saints from Paul to Thomas More were the genuinely thoughtful promised any other lot, whether at the hands of the world or at the hands of their uncomprehending brethren, than contradiction and constant testing?

Finally, and urgently, there is an intensely practical problem in this matter of American Catholic intellectual life. It is the problem of how we can increase the proportions of authentic scholars and trained, competent intellectuals among us.

Statistics have been offered recently which point up and analyze the dearth of Catholic lay scholars. These statistics have been challenged by those who resented certain of its implications, although their resentment did not inspire much in the way of effective refutation of the facts. The facts add up to a conclusion which is a primary justification for the republication of this present paper, by a man who dearly loves the Faith and is one of those who spare themselves nothing to contribute to the solution of whatever problems impede the freedom and well-being of our Holy Mother the Church.

In the early days of the Church in America, humble Catholics struggled to retain the Faith in an anti-Catholic atmosphere. These early pioneers built schools and churches which are responsible for the survival of Catholic America today. These foundations for growth and expansion have been firmly rooted within the American tradition in our soil, but future progress and expansion will come only through a determined effort based upon the development of Catholic scholarship. It is to this problem that Monsignor Ellis addresses himself so effectively, and we recommend a reading and rereading of his provocative message at periodic and regular intervals. We have a need for an "Apostolate of distinction."

+ John Wright
Bishop of Worcester

Contents

American Catholics
and the Intellectual Life

JOHN TRACY ELLIS

WITHIN THE LAST YEAR the role of the intellectual in American society has been submitted to a searching scrutiny rarely if ever before witnessed in this country. Some of these critiques, such as the comments of Russell Kirk and Clinton Rossiter, have been more immediately concerned with the relation of the intellectual to what has been termed the "new conservatism."[1] The greater number, however, have taken a broader view, and have sought to trace the causes for the anti-intellectual temper of our society, and to suggest ways

---

[1] Russell Kirk, "Ethical Labor," *Sewanee Review,* LXII (Summer, 1954), 485–503; Clinton Rossiter, "Toward an American Conservatism," *Yale Review,* XLIV (Spring, 1955), 354–372.

that will enable the intellectual to move out of the isolated and suspect position to which so many of his fellow citizens have assigned
him. In this latter category mention might be made of the stimulating essays of Francis G. Wilson, Philip Blair Rice, Robert F. Fitch,
Henry Steele Commager, John U. Nef, and Merle Curti.[2] The authors of all these articles are themselves intellectuals. The sincerity
with which they approach their task is manifest, and the loyalty
which they demonstrate to the highest ideals of their profession will
prove heartening to anyone who has chosen a vocation to the intellectual life. Their analysis reveals a universal agreement that the
situation of the intellectual in the United States has been, and is, at
the present time, deplorable. But what gives to the observations of
these scholars a truly refreshing quality is the healthy spirit of self-
criticism which most of them display. In general one may say that
there is among them a fundamental agreement with the judgment
of Commager when he remarks of the American intellectuals, "They
have failed to enlist the great mass of their countrymen in the common cultural and intellectual enterprise necessary for the Republic's
progress and security."[3]

---

[2]Francis G. Wilson, "Public Opinion and the Intellectuals," *American
Political Science Review,* XLVIII (June, 1954), 321–339; Philip Blair
Rice, "The Intellectual Quarterly in a Non-Intellectual Society," *Ken-
yon Review,* XVI (Summer, 1954), 420–439; Robert F. Fitch, "The
Fears of the Intelligentsia. The Present Slough of Despond," *Commen-
tary,* XVIII (October, 1954), 328–335; Henry Steele Commager, "Why
Are We Mad at Teacher?", *The Reporter,* XI (October 21, 1954),
39–41; John U. Nef, "The Significance of *The Review of Politics,*"
XVII (January, 1955), 24–32; Merle Curti, "Intellectuals and Other
People," *American Historical Review,* LX (January, 1955), 259–282.

[3]*Op. cit.,* p. 41. A recent article by an assistant professor of sociology
in Haverford College maintains—contrary to common belief—that the
position of the intellectual has of late been enhanced by reason of a
kind of artistic and intellectual renaissance taking place in the United
States that has brought natural and social scientists, as well as academicians in business and government, a more respected status. Writers like

In view of this fact, therefore, the subject of the historical record of American Catholics in intellectual affairs is a very timely one. For the position of the Catholic intellectual in the United States is not basically different from that of his non-Catholic colleague. In fact, in some ways it may even be worse. In any case, nothing but good can result for all who are concerned with this problem from a discussion of the historic background and present status of the Catholic intellectual, especially when the discussion is conducted in the same candid and critical spirit that has characterized the writings to which reference has been made.

Fourteen years ago one of the most perceptive of living foreign observers of American life and institutions, Denis W. Brogan, professor of political science in the University of Cambridge, stated in a book on the United States: ". . . in no Western society is the intellectual prestige of Catholicism lower than in the country where,

---

Russell Lynes, David Riesman, and Jacques Barzun are quoted as believing that the current attacks on the intellectuals indicate the growing importance of the latter, and the fear of those who dislike them that they are really having an increasing influence in American life. This author states: "As I have indicated, my own informal observations would lead me to support the thesis presented by Lynes, by Riesman, and by Barzun: namely, that the general status of the intellectual is high and that he currently rides the wave of mass distributed culture which sweeps up the beaches of the American middle class."—Milton M. Gordon, "Social Class and American Intellectuals," *American Association of University Professors Bulletin*, XL (Winter, 1954–55), 522–523. In the same issue of the *Bulletin*, Wilson Record, assistant professor of sociology in Sacramento State College, analyzes the reasons and motivation that led so many American intellectuals into the camp of the communists and leftists during the 1930's, a trend which had much to do with lessening the regard for intellectuals generally on the part of the American public. Record would not seem to share Gordon's optimism about the progress made of late. He says, "The intellectual is *in* American culture, but he is not *of* it in the sense of playing a well-defined role that is continuously reinforced by a feeling of 'belonging.' " —"The American Intellectual as Black Sheep and Red Rover," *Ibid.*, XL (Winter, 1954–55), 537.

in such respects as wealth, numbers, and strength of organization, it is so powerful."[4] No well-informed American Catholic will attempt to challenge that statement. Admittedly, the weakest aspect of the Church in this country lies in its failure to produce national leaders and to exercise commanding influence in intellectual circles, and this at a time when the number of Catholics in the United States is exceeded only by those of Brazil and Italy, and their material resources are incomparably superior to those of any other branch of the universal Church. What, one may ask, is the explanation of this striking discrepancy? The remainder of this paper will be devoted to an attempt to answer that question by a development of certain major points based, for the most part, on the history of the American Church.

The first point, namely, the implanting in this soil of a deep anti-Catholic prejudice by the original English settlers in the early seventeenth century, requires no elaborate proof for any educated American. One has but to read the exhaustive monograph of Sister Mary Augustina Ray, B.V.M., on eighteenth-century America, or the general work of Gustavus Myers,[5] to understand how thoroughly hostile to all things Catholic great numbers of Americans have always been, and the pains that they have taken to perpetuate that bias since it first entered the stream of American history at Jamestown and Plymouth Rock. In the spring of 1942 I had the fact brought home to me in a forceful way when Professor Arthur M. Schlesinger, Sr., of Harvard University, one of the outstanding authorities in American social history, remarked to me during a friendly chat in Cambridge, "I regard the bias against your Church

---

[4]D. W. Brogan, *U.S.A. An Outline of the Country, Its People and Institutions* (London, 1941), p. 65.

[5]Sister Mary Augustina Ray, B.V.M., *American Opinion of Roman Catholicism in the Eighteenth Century* (New York, 1936); Gustavus Myers, *History of Bigotry in the United States* (New York, 1943).

as the most persistent prejudice in the history of the American people." Any notion that this sentiment was only a part of our past has been thoroughly dispelled by the substantial support afforded to groups like the Protestants and Other Americans United for Separation of Church and State since World War II.

Historically speaking, therefore, the American intellectual climate has been aloof and unfriendly to Catholic thought and ideas, when it has not been openly hostile, and it places no burden upon the imagination to appreciate how this factor has militated against a strong and vibrant intellectual life among the Catholics of this country. All but the most sanguine of men feel discouragement in circumstances of this kind and the majority usually give way to the natural tendency to slacken their efforts. What is more serious, the presence of so widespread a prejudice among the great majority of the population prompts the minority to withdraw into itself and to assume the attitude of defenders of a besieged fortress. That this situation had such an effect on many Catholics, there is no doubt. Even so brave and talented a man as John Carroll, the first American Catholic bishop, revealed the timidity engendered among the Catholics of his day by hatred of their Church when he was compelled to go into print in 1784 to refute a subtle attack on Catholic doctrine from the first American apostate priest. As Carroll remarked, "I could not forget, in the beginning, progress, and conclusion of it, that the habits of thinking, the prejudices, perhaps even the passions of many of my readers, would be set against all the arguments I could offer. . . ."[6] How many Catholics since Carroll's day could attest to the same reluctance when they sought to exercise their talents in behalf of Catholic truth? And yet anti-Catholic bias should not be advanced as the prime factor in this situation. More damaging than its direct effect on the intellectual

---

[6]Peter Guilday, *The Life and Times of John Carroll, Archbishop of Baltimore, 1735–1815* (New York, 1922), I, 126.

shortcomings of American Catholics, has probably been the fostering by this historic bias of an overeagerness in Catholic circles for
apologetics rather than pure scholarship.

A second major consideration which helps to account for the
failure of American Catholics to make a notable mark upon the
intellectual life of their country is the character and background of
the major portion of the people who, until a relatively recent date,
made up the Church in the United States. From the 1820's, when
the Irish began immigrating to the new world in large numbers, to
the 1920's, when Congress locked the doors upon all but a small
proportion of the immigrants who sought these shores, the Catholic
Church was faced with the staggering task of absorbing an estimated
9,317,000 immigrants of its faith.[7] We do not need to be told what
the immigrant status implied by way of poverty, hardship, yes, and
even illiteracy. Most of us learned it from tales told by our grandparents within the intimacy of the family circle. And since we have
had the advantage of a finished education and know what that requires, we can easily understand how impossible it was for our
ancestors to produce anything approaching a thriving intellectual
life. Moreover, the grave responsibility that these unceasing waves
of immigrants imposed upon the leaders of the Church to see that
they had the rudiments of religious instruction and the facilities for
Mass and the sacraments, left little time, funds, or leisure for a
more highly cultivated training. Brogan understands that fact. In
1941 he wrote:

> Not until this generation has the Church been given time
> (with the cessation of mass immigration) to take breath and
> take stock. One result of this preoccupation with the immi-
> grants has been that the Catholic Church in America has

---

[7]Gerald Shaughnessy, S.M., *Has the Immigrant Kept the Faith?* (New
York, 1925), pp. 113–196, contains the most accurate data available
for the Catholic population trends from 1820 to 1920.

counted for astonishingly little in the formation of the American intellectual climate. . . .[8]

It is only the exceptional man—for example, John Gilmary Shea,[9] the historian of the American Church—who can make headway in the world of scholarship amid crippling poverty and the harassing anxiety of providing a living for himself and his dependents. That was the lot of most of the Catholics in this country in Shea's generation and before, and that there should have resulted a pitifully meager record of accomplishment in the things of the mind is thus quite understandable.

But even if the energies of the American Catholic body down to a generation ago had not been so completely absorbed in the primary duty of assimilating the millions of immigrants, any true intellectual distinction—had it been there—would have met with very slight appreciation in the United States. Historically Americans have been wary of their scholars, and it is doubtful if there is a major nation in the world whose history reveals more suspicion of its academicians than our own. It is now 120 years since de Tocqueville published his famous book on American institutions, and among his many wise observations he stated:

> In the United States the people do not hate the higher classes of society, but are not favorably inclined towards them and carefully exclude them from the exercise of authority. They do not fear distinguished talents, but are rarely fond of them. In general, everyone who rises without their aid seldom obtains their favor.[10]

---

[8]Brogan, *op. cit.*, p. 65.

[9]For a pathetic account of the poverty he experienced and the lack of support given to Shea during the writing of his great four-volume *History of the Catholic Church in the United States* (New York, 1886–1892), ch. the correspondence reprinted in Peter Guilday, "John Gilmary Shea," *Historical Records and Studies*, XVII (July, 1926), 81–146.

[10]Alexis de Tocqueville, *Democracy in America,* edited by Phillips Bradley (New York, 1945), I, 202.

The prevalence of this egalitarian spirit and the leveling process which it inspired prompted Orestes Brownson to inveigh against the American practice of dethroning all distinction when he delivered the commencement address at Mount Saint Mary's College in 1853. On that occasion he pleaded with the graduates to resist with might and main this tendency which he characterized as "the grand heresy of our age."[11] Nor have matters greatly improved since the time of de Tocqueville and Brownson, for it has been our own generation that has given birth to the terms "brain trusters" and "egg heads" to designate the popular concept of professors who have descended from Mount Olympus to engage actively in the realm of public affairs.

In this respect, I regret to say, I can see no appreciable difference between the attitudes assumed by American Catholics and those commonly held among their fellow countrymen of other religious faiths. The historian looks in vain—always excepting the lonely few—for a higher evaluation and a more understanding attitude toward the pursuits of the mind among those who are Catholics in this country. In that—as in so many other ways—the Catholics are, and have been, thoroughly American, and they have shown no more marked disposition to foster scholarship and to honor intellectual achievement than have any other group. In this their European coreligionists have often been far in advance of them. One recalls, for example, the splendid efforts made by the Belgian hierachy, their priests and people, in rallying so bravely—and so successfully—behind Rector Pierre F.-X. de Ram and his colleagues in 1834 in restoring the great Catholic University of Lou-

---

[11]Henry F. Brownson (ed.), *The Works of Orestes A. Brownson* (Detroit, 1885), XIX, 439. The title of the address was "Liberal Studies," and it was delivered on June 29, 1853, before the Philomathian Society. Among the six graduates of that year were the future artist, John LaFarge, and the later fifth Bishop of Vincennes, Silas M. Chatard.

vain. In terms of the comparative attitudes of many American and European Catholics to matters of this kind, it would be gratifying to record that the Catholics of the United States were an exception to the witty extravagance of a certain dean who once remarked that "in the Old World an ordinary mortal on seeing a professor tipped his hat while in America he tapped his head."[12] But, alas, as far as my reading and observation enable me to speak, I find no grounds for the exception.

One of the principal reasons for the lack of such an exception is, I think, the absence of an intellectual tradition among American Catholics. Obviously the establishment of such a tradition was impossible amid the stifling persecution and discrimination which Catholics experienced in colonial America. With the dawn of religious liberty after the American Revolution there was a brief span of years when it seemed that a tradition of this kind was slowly taking root among the families of the Maryland Catholic gentry. For the personal wealth of some of these families like the Carrolls, the Neales, and the Brookes, along with their deep and ardent Catholic faith, had enabled them to send their children to Europe where they acquired an education that was second to none among Americans of their generation. Moreover, when the French Revolution had turned violently anticlerical in the 1790's there came to this country a large number of highly cultivated French priests who exercised a strong and uplifting influence upon the intellectual life of the small and beleaguered Catholic body. One has but to recall the names of François Matigon, Jean Cheverus, Simon Bruté, Benedict Flaget, and Gabriel Richard—all men of a finished education, fine personal libraries, and a deep love of learning—to know what is meant. But before this high promise of the early nineteenth century had time to attain fulfillment the arrival of the great mass

---

[12]Merle Curti, "Intellectuals and Other People," *American Historical Review,* LX (January, 1955), 259.

of immigrants dissipated the early hope for intellectual distinction which faded away before the all-important task of saving souls.

As the mid-century approached, it is true, there came another ray of hope when a small band of intellectual converts afforded a temporary expectation that the American Church might witness an Oxford Movement of its own. Within the single decade of the 1840's Orestes Brownson, Augustine Hewit, Isaac Hecker, Anna Hanson Dorsey, George Allen, Clarence Walworth, James Roosevelt Bayley, Jedidiah Huntington, William Henry Anderson, and Joseph Chandler found their way into the Church. They were all native-born Americans of prominent families, most of them had received the best American education of their time in predominantly Protestant schools, and practically all of them were of a literary turn of mind and might be termed intellectuals. They did, indeed, lift the intellectual tone of Catholicism in this country. But the predominant cast had already been given to the religious society they now entered, and the fact that in the decade of their conversion the immigrant population accounted for 700,000 out of the 1,606,000 Catholics in the country by 1850, would explain in good measure the relatively slight impression which this little band of converts made upon the intellectual life of the vast majority of their coreligionists. With the latter the all-absorbing ambition was to find a livelihood and to make the minimum of necessary adjustments to their new environment. In the end the native-born converts with their thoroughly American background were no more successful than the European-educated and European-born Catholics of an earlier generation in establishing a lasting intellectual tradition.

It was the conviction of the need for a tradition of this kind in the American Church that inspired some of the finest passages of the sermon preached by John Lancaster Spalding, Bishop of Peoria, during the Third Plenary Council of Baltimore. To Spalding the time was long overdue for the Catholics of this country to stand forth and give the lie to the inherited prejudice of millions of Americans that the Church was the mother of ignorance. Catholic conduct during the nation's wars, he remarked, had convinced all but the most unreasonable of the depth and sincerity of their patriotism. But in the intellectual order, it was another matter. Thus said Spalding:

> when our zeal for intellectual excellence shall have raised up men who will take place among the first writers and thinkers of their day their very presence will become the most persuasive of arguments to teach the world that no best gift is at war with the spirit of Catholic faith. . . .[13]

Five years later at the centennial of the American hierarchy John Ireland, Archbishop of St. Paul, made a similar plea to the Catholics of the United States to strive for leadership in intellectual circles. He stated:

> This is an intellectual age. It worships intellect. It tries all things by the touchstone of intellect. . . . The Church herself will be judged by the standard of intellect. Catholics must excel in religious knowledge. . . . They must be in the foreground of intellectual movements of all kinds. The age will not take kindly to religious knowledge separated from secular knowledge.[14]

---

[13]John Lancaster Spalding, *Means and Ends of Education* (Chicago, 1897), p. 220. Spalding entitled the sermon preached on November 16, 1884, "Higher Education."

[14]John Ireland, *The Church and Modern Society* (St. Paul, 1905), I, 92. The title of Ireland's sermon preached on November 10, 1889, was "The Mission of Catholics in America." A recent example of a similar exhortation to the Catholics of Asia resulted from the Asia Seminar of Pax Romana held in Madras, India, in December, 1954. ". . . a genuine Catholic intellectual," it was said, "tries finally to see whether he can reach what in his particular case would be the highest and most fruitful form of his apostolate: i.e. to bring the presence of Christ and the Church by his own competence as a Catholic into even the loftiest fields of human intellectual endeavour. . . . It should anyway be made

Yet in spite of the stirring pleas of bishops like Spalding and Ireland, and of the constant and heroic efforts of editors like Brownson in his *Quarterly Review,* of Hecker in the *Catholic World,* and of James A. Corcoran in the *American Catholic Quarterly Review,* the vast majority of Catholics remained relatively impervious to the intellectual movements of their time. A fact which demonstrates clearly the failure of an intellectual tradition to have taken root among them up to the closing years of the last century relates to the Catholic University of America. When the American hierarchy opened the University in November, 1889, the native-born Catholics of this country were so devoid of scholarly distinction that the first rector, John J. Keane, was compelled to recruit his original faculty of eight men from among six foreign-born professors and two American-born converts.[15] One could scarcely find

---

quite clear that, while the oft and justly condemned temporal and materialistic *exclusive* outlook stands indeed as the enemy number one of modern and of all civilization, it is also quite as unchristian to seek refuge in a kind of spiritual ghetto, and through a mistaken type of angelism to ignore the deep significance of and our duty towards temporal values. Such an attitude of absenteeism and of manichean or escapist laissez faire is philosophically wrong in relation to the full meaning of the human person, and theologically not admissible, to put it mildly. It has unhappily contributed to foster many a positive misgiving concerning the so-called conflict between science and religion, the earthly city and the heavenly Kingdom. Some consider it the tragedy, to a large extent, of late modern Christianity in the West."—E. Ugarte, S.J., "Future Catholics in Modern Asia & the Pax Romana Asia Seminar," *Clergy Monthly,* XIX (March, 1955), 197.

[15]John Tracy Ellis, *The Formative Years of the Catholic University of America* (Washington, 1946), pp. 371–373. The foreign-born were Joseph Schroeder (dogmatic theology), Thomas Bouquillon (moral theology), Henri Hyvernat (scripture and Oriental languages), Joseph Pohle (philosophy), George M. Searle (astronomy and physics), John B. Hogan (president of Divinity College); the American-born converts were Charles Warren Stoddard (English literature) and Augustine F. Hewit (church history). Constrasting the dependence of American

a more striking illustration of intellectual impoverishment than this, especially when it is remembered that Bishop Keane had sought in every way possible to avoid the charge of "foreignism" which groups like the A.P.A. were then leveling against his infant institution.

One of the main reasons why the American Church after a century of organized existence in the United States found itself with no intellectual tradition was, I am convinced again, due to the character and background of its adherents. Had there been a sufficiently large number of American Catholic families with several generations of a solid tradition and love of learning in their midst, the appeals of men like Brownson and Spalding might, indeed, have borne more fruit. The LaFarge family is a case in point. In the correspondence of John LaFarge, the artist, during his school days at Mount Saint Mary's College in Emmitsburg one finds, for example, that before LaFarge had reached his sixteenth birthday he had in the course of two and a half months requested his father to send him works of Herodotus, Plautus, Catullus, Theocritus, Dryden, Goldsmith, Michelet, Molière, Corneille, and Victor Hugo.[16] And that the love of books acquired by the great artist was passed on to his children, was recently witnessed when his Jesuit son published his interesting memoirs and described how seriously reading was taken in the LaFarge household. There his uncle,

---

scholarship upon Europe up to a generation ago and the change that has taken place since, Merle Curti has remarked, "But the striking fact has been the gradual reversal in the debtor-creditor relationship between American and European scholars."—Merle Curti (Ed.), *American Scholarship in the Twentieth Century* (Cambridge, 1953), p. 5. The chapter in this volume entitled "Historical Scholarship" by W. Stull Holt (pp. 83–110) canvasses practically every aspect of history writing in the United States since 1900 but ignores developments in church history entirely.

[16]"Schoolboy Letters between John LaFarge and His Father," *Historical Records and Studies*, XVIII (March, 1938), 74–120.

Thomas Sergeant Perry, professor of English at Harvard, his father, and his mother read regularly to the children from the best books. Out of habits such as these there developed a taste for good literature and Father LaFarge tells us:

> One day in August when I was about thirteen, I finished devouring Boswell's *Life of Johnson* and a feeling of desolation came over me as I turned the last page. . . . Then the bright idea occurred to me, why not read the two fat volumes through again? It was a wise choice and I shall never regret it.[17]

That is the kind of background from which true intellectuals are born, but how many American Catholic families are there of whom that could be said? This is what John J. Wynne, S.J., had in mind when he discussed with Monsignor Edward A. Pace in the letters they exchanged early in this century the need for stimulating Catholics to read. As Wynne remarked on one occasion, the habit of reading must be started in the home. "We must, therefore, devise some means," he said, "of inculcating this habit in the homes of our people; otherwise we shall be providing books for our own bookshelves or for the libraries of a small number of priests and a few seminaries."[18]

It is a sad fact but, I think, a true one that on the whole American Catholic families have largely failed in this regard, just as the families of Americans generally have failed. The tradition that established itself in the LaFarge family circle has never enjoyed wide acceptance in Catholic households, and when an attempt to foster such a tradition is sometimes made in Catholic institutions

---

[17]John LaFarge, S.J., *The Manner Is Ordinary* (New York, 1954), p. 40.

[18]Archives of the Catholic University of America, Pace Papers, Wynne to Pace, New York, March 16, 1914.

of higher education it is often found that the effort has come too late.

But the lack of serious reading habits is not the only national characteristic which the Catholics of the United States have thoroughly imbibed. From the time when the Duc de Liancourt traveled through the states along the eastern seaboard in the 1790's and wrote one of the earliest books by a foreigner on the new Republic, to the essays of recent observers like Evelyn Waugh, few visitors from abroad have neglected to comment on the American attachment to material goods and the desire to make a fortune as dominant characteristics of our society. One is reminded of the emphasis that Plato gave to this point when he said that "in proportion as riches and rich men are honoured in the State, virtue and the virtuous are dishonoured. And what is honoured is cultivated, and that which has no honour is neglected."[19] That this has been true from the beginning of our national life was the burden of some of the finest chapters of Henry Adams' famous *History*. Speaking of New England, where one might expect to find the best that the young Republic had to offer, Adams said:

> The intellectual wants of the community grew with the growing prosperity; but the names of half-a-dozen persons could hardly be mentioned whose memories survived by intellectual work made public in Massachusetts between 1783 and 1800.[20]

If that was true of the green wood of New England Protestantism after a century or more of Harvard and Yale, what was one to say of the dry in the small and despised community of American Catholocism? Moreover, time saw no improvement for, as Adams

---

[19]*The Republic,* translated by B. Jowett (New York, n.d.), p. 301.

[20]Henry Adams, *History of the United States of America* (New York, 1891), I, 93.

noted, the more the seemingly inexhaustible riches of this vast land were unearthed, the more fixed did the American ideal of wealth become in the national mind. The fact lent plausibility to Brownson's indictment at the mid-century when he deplored the dethroning of every vestige of true aristocracy and distinction as a result of the French revolutions of 1789, 1830, and 1848, to which he added:

> Such are rapidly becoming our own American nobility, or aristocracy. Our gentlemen are bankers, sharpers, brokers, stock-jobbers, traders, speculators, attorneys, pettifoggers, and in general worshippers of mammon.[21]

As far as I can see, it would be difficult to maintain that the picture has changed essentially since Brownson wrote his trenchant lines in 1853.

Here, too, the prevailing American ethos took captive the Catholics as well as those affiliated with other churches. In no single phase of national life have Catholics made the contribution to leadership which might be expected of them, but if there be any exception to this general statement, it almost certainly lies in the field of business. For example, six years ago William Miller of Harvard made a study of 187 business leaders and 163 political leaders for the first ten years of the twentieth century. In neither category were the Catholics distinguished, but it is worthy of note that they comprised almost double (7 per cent) the number of leaders in business that they did in politics (4 per cent) during the years 1900–1910.[22] A similar investigation by Liston Pope, professor of social ethics in Yale University, which centered around the years 1939–1946 tended to bear out the same conclusion. In

---

[21]Brownson, *op. cit.*, XIX, 439.

[22]William Miller, "American Historians and the Business Elite," *Journal of Economic History*, IX (November, 1949), 203.

this case a scrutiny of the relation between the religious affiliation and economic status of Protestants and Catholics at the opening of the 1940's led to the equally interesting observation that "Protestantism had a larger representation from the lower class and Catholicism had more middle-class members than popular generalizations have assumed."[23] In other words, Catholics have moved up the economic ladder beyond the rung where popular impression had placed them.

I was sufficiently intrigued by the data contained in these articles to institute an investigation among the students of my seminar on the subject of Catholic leadership in the three fields of business, politics, and scholarship during the 1940's. Their findings were, of course, quite tentative in nature, but they did indicate that, relatively speaking, Catholic business leadership on a national scale in those years ran ahead of leadership in national politics, and it made the showing by Catholics who had attained national recognition through productive scholarship seem insignificant by comparison.[24]

---

[23]Liston Pope, "Religion and the Class Structure," *Annals of the American Academy of Political and Social Science,* CCLVI (March, 1948), 85–86. Pope's study was based in part on Hadley Cantril, "Educational and Economic Compositions of Religious Groups," *American Journal of Sociology,* XLVII (March, 1943), 574–579.

[24]The investigations were made by Father Bosco Cestello, O.S.B., Father Oderic Foley, O.F.M.Conv., and Mother Mary Peter Carthy, O.S.U. Their studies were conducted on the basis of the names found in such standard works as *Who's Who in America, Directory of American Scholars, Who's Who in Commerce and Industry,* and the *American Catholic Who's Who.* It was found, for example, that there were 171 Catholic businessmen in positions of the first rank—predominantly in manufacturing and banking and finance—for the years investigated; whereas in the entire history of the country there have been only five Catholic members of the Supreme Court of the United States and fourteen members of the Presidents' cabinets out of a total of 301 men since 1789, and ten of these have been appointed since 1933. In 1943 there were fifty-nine Catholic members out of the total of 435 in the House of Representatives and ten among the ninety-six members of the United

There is, then, warrant for saying that Catholics have not only shown an increasing participation in the native penchant for making money, but that, all things considered, they have probably attained more distinction in the business world than they have in any other sector of American life.[25]

But has the arrival of a fairly large number of American Catholic businessmen at the status of millionaires—many of whom are college graduates—occasioned any notable change in their attitude toward or increase in their support of the intellectual pursuits of

---

States Senate. The tentative conclusions concerning distinction among the American Catholics in scholarship in the 1940's (only lay Catholics who had published contributions in their respective specialties were counted) indicated generally a poorer showing than those in business and politics.

[25]In this connection the recent monograph of Irving G. Wyllie, *The Self-Made Man in America. The Myth of Rags to Riches* (New Brunswick, 1954), reaches an interesting, if not altogether convincing conclusion. Speaking of the glorification of big businessmen and huge fortunes by leading Protestant ministers of the early twentieth century, Wyllie remarks that "of the well-known clergy who pointed the way to wealth, none was a Roman Catholic." He sees the reason for this in the fact that prior to 1900 never more than 7 per cent of the business elite were Catholics and less than 10 per cent of them were foreign-born. Wyllie then concludes: "In ministering to immigrants in the years after the Civil War, and especially to those from southern and eastern Europe, the Catholic Church was working with men who had very little chance of achieving outstanding financial success. In addition, by standing aloof from the glorification of wealth, Catholic spokesmen upheld their church's traditional indictment of materialism" (pp. 56–57). Wyllie neglects to say that the Church never indicted the accumulation of a fortune, provided it was honestly made and properly spent. If Catholic churchmen refrained from extolling wealth after the manner of Henry Ward Beecher, Lyman Abbot, and their kind, they found nothing incongruous in having the Church benefit from these fortunes as, for example, when Archbishop Ireland opened the St. Paul Seminary in September, 1894, made possible by the gift of $500,000 from James J. Hill, President of the Great Northern Railroad.

their coreligionists? That question brings us to the sixth major point which I should like to make, namely, the failure of Catholics in posts of leadership, both clerical and lay, to understand fully, or to appreciate in a practical way, the value of the vocation of the intellectual. First, to return to the question of the laity, the answer is not, I believe, a clear Yes or an unqualified No. About the only norm of judgment that one can apply to their attitude, unless one knows them personally, is their outward action in the form of endowments of the things of the mind. In that respect one can say that the situation at present reveals a higher appreciation of intellectual values on the part of Catholics of wealth than it did two generations ago when, to be sure, the number possessing large fortunes was much smaller. To cite once more the history of my own University, with which I am best acquainted, I think it was somewhat significant that when the committee of the hierarchy sought funds for the institution in the 1880's they received only two gifts of really large size, the sum of $300,000 from Miss Mary Gwendolyn Caldwell and $100,000 from Eugene Kelly of New York. Moreover, in the sixty-six years that the University has been in existence there have not been more than about ten instances where bequests of $100,000 or more have been received from individual American Catholics of wealth, and in only one case did the amount approach the million mark when the residue of the estate of Theodore B. Basselin, who died in April 1914, brought to the University nearly $900,000 for the endowment of scholarships for students studying for the priesthood.

But if the Catholic University of America has not been especially fortunate in this regard, in recent years some of its sister institutions have fared better. To mention only a few examples, the College of St. Thomas and the University of Notre Dame have benefited handsomely from the generosity of Ignatius A. O'Shaughnessy, Loyola University, Chicago, from that of Francis J. Lewis, and Mount Saint Mary's College, Emmitsburg, and Notre Dame from a like generosity on the part of Thomas W. Pangborn. All things considered, the last two decades have seen improvement in the financial support given to intellectual enterprises by Catholics of wealth in this country. Furthermore, the current awareness which many American business leaders are demonstrating of their responsibility toward higher education is a happy augury, and it gives rise to the hope that the Catholics among them will now step forward and identify themselves strongly with this movement. The Knights of Columbus have given them a splendid example by their recent gift to Saint Louis University for the microfilming of the manuscripts in the Vatican Library, a benefaction which will prove of inestimable value to the prestige and future possibilities of American Catholic scholarship. To date, however, it may be truly said that the over-all record of intelligent appreciation and high evaluation for the intellectual activities of their Church on the part of wealthy Catholic lay leaders has not been an impressive one.

While on the subject of the laity's role in matters of this kind it is pertinent to observe that whatever assistance wealthy Catholic laymen may see fit to give to the advancement of scholarship in the Church's institutions of higher learning will, in good measure, redound to the benefit of their fellow laymen far more than it will to the clergy. The percentage of lay teachers at every level of American Catholic education has been steadily increasing of late years, and this is especially true of the colleges and universities. For example, in the academic year 1952–1953 laymen composed 73.8 per cent of the entire faculty of the Catholic University of America,[26] and in the same year of 753 members of the teaching staff of Marquette University 700 were drawn from the laity.[27] This

---

[26]"News from the Field," *Catholic Educational Review,* LI (November, 1953), 638.

[27]*Annual School Report. Archdiocese of Milwaukee, 1952–1953* (Milwaukee, 1953), p. 33.

situation is entirely as it should be, for the layman and laywoman have an important part to play in the educational enterprises of the Church and, in fact, Catholic scholarship and learning, generally speaking, would be improved by giving to the laity more of a voice in the shaping of educational policy and in the active administration of the Catholic colleges and universities of the United States.[28]

That brings us to the role played by the clerical leaders of the American Church. In anything that is said or written on the subject of either the clerical or lay leaders in the Church of the United States it should be constantly kept in mind that, *mutatis mutandis,* the vast majority of them have been men of their own generation, reflecting—apart from the dogmatic and moral views which they held as Catholics—the predominant attitudes and prevailing tendencies of their time. Thus the solemn dignity and stately bearing of Archbishop Carroll suggested the eighteenth-century gentleman of Washington's generation in a way that might even seem a trifle stuffy to a twentieth-century prelate. Again, the bold and somewhat raucous utterances of a Bishop England and an Archbishop Hughes, faced as they were by the virulent attacks on their immigrant flocks during the era of nativism and the Know-Nothings, would probably appear out of place to Bishop Russell and Cardinal Farley, their successors in the Sees of Charleston and New York

---

[28]For a study of the role of the laity in the intellectual pursuits of the Church from the viewpoint of canon law cf. Alexander O. Sigur, "Lay Cooperation with the Magisterium," *The Jurist,* XIII (July, 1953), 268–297. Nearly a century ago the writer of an unsigned article in one of the leading Catholic journals anticipated the day when there would be Catholic colleges conducted by laymen. He said: "A new order of Catholic colleges, with lay professors of acknowledged merit, similar in this respect to the other universities of the country will, ere long, arise and afford still greater variety and perhaps means for more extended study and deeper research, if indeed the time has yet come for them in this country."—"The Catholic Element in the History of the United States," *The Metropolitan,* V (August, 1857), 526.

forty years ago, when the Church had by that time entered upon
an age of impressive strength and security. In the same sense the
bishops and major superiors of the religious orders of this generation reveal, it seems to me, the characteristics of their time, for
among them one will find men whose executive and administrative
talents are of a very high order. It is fortunate that this is so, for
it is no exaggeration to say that the Catholic Church of the United
States has become "big business" in the typically American meaning of that term. And, we may add, woe to Catholic interests if the
bishops and the heads of the principal religious orders were not
men who possessed the ability to cope with the problems that the
far-flung commitments of the American Church now daily impose
upon them![29]

Yet it is to be regretted that the pressing tasks of administration
leave so little time and leisure to these spiritual superiors for a
more active participation and effective encouragement to intellectual concerns. Their backgrounds do not account for the lack of it,
for they are basically the same as that of the Catholic intellectuals
themselves. That point was made clear by Archbishop Cushing in
1947 when he stated to the ninth annual convention of the C.I.O.
meeting in his see city:

> I have said this before, but it is important to repeat it here:
> in all the American hierarchy, resident in the United States,
> there is not known to me one Bishop, Archbishop or Cardinal
> whose father or mother was a college graduate. Every one of
> our Bishops and Archbishops is the son of a working man and
> a working man's wife.[30]

Many of these prelates of whom the Archbishop of Boston spoke
are, of course, themselves college graduates, and a considerable

---

[29]The economic and social backgrounds of the American hierarchy
would afford the basis for a very worthwhile study.

[30]Boston *Pilot,* October 17, 1947. The archbishop's speech was delivered at the opening session on October 13.

number of them are the products of graduate training in fields like theology, philosophy, canon law, education, and social work. To be sure, these are not *per se* fields of vocational training, but there has been a strong tendency to make them that. On the other hand, relatively few of the higher clergy have taken graduate work in the humanities and the liberal arts. As a consequence one will find among them, I believe, a far greater emphasis on what are the professional and vocational aspects of higher education, since they serve a practical end in their diocesan chanceries, charities, and offices of the superintendents of schools, than might otherwise be the case. In this, I submit, they faithfully mirror the intense preoccupation of American leaders in all walks of life with the practical. That the practical order of things is of vital importance to the Church, no one with any understanding of its mission would attempt to deny. But by the same token the Church has a mission to the intellectual elite and this, I fear, has been allowed to suffer neglect by reason of the prevalence of the practical.

Apart, however, from personal backgrounds, the harassing day-to-day duties of administration, and the national temper of practicality which bishops and religious superiors—like all the rest of us—have imbibed as an influencing factor in their lives, the churchmen have not been able to draw upon a well-established intellectual tradition inherited from the countries of their origin. The majority of these men have been of Irish or German extraction, and by virtue of similarity of language and customs many of them have closely followed developments of the Church in England. In neither the Ireland nor the Germany of their grandparents and parents, nor in the England that they have observed since the conversion of Newman in 1845, have they found such a tradition. For example, when Dr. Newman attempted to carry out the vague and often contradictory directives of the Irish hierarchy for a Catholic university in the 1850's, we all know how miserably he failed. Nearly seventy years after Newman had left Dublin in deep discouragement the distinguished English Benedictine historian, Cuthbert Butler, wrote of his own father's close association with Newman during the elder Butler's years as professor of mathematics in the Catholic University of Ireland. Quoting his father, Butler said:

> His view was that . . . the Irish bishops, not having themselves had a University education, did not properly understand what it was, and, with one or two exceptions, did not really want such a University as Newman had in mind; their idea was a glorified Seminary for the laity. . . .[31]

Nor could the American bishops fall back upon any strong tradition in England or Germany. The fiasco of Cardinal Manning's ill-starred University College at Kensington in the 1870's was so complete that the permission granted in 1895 for Catholics to attend Oxford and Cambridge might almost be viewed as a belated consolation for the humiliation and loss of prestige which they had experienced for so long a time in English intellectual circles.[32] In the German world conditions were better, but still left much to be desired. The repeated efforts of certain intellectuals to rally their

---

[31]Cuthbert Butler, O.S.B., *The Life and Times of Bishop Ullathorne, 1806–1889* (New York, 1926), II, 312, n. 1. For the full story of Newman's failure cf. the scholarly work of Fergal McGrath, S.J., *Newman's University. Idea and Reality* (London, 1951).

[32]On University College, Kensington, cf. Edmund Sheridan Purcell, *Life of Cardinal Manning* (New York, 1896), II, 495–505; on the question of the Catholics at Oxford and Cambridge cf. H. O. Evennett's chapter, "Catholics and the Universities," in George Andrew Beck, A.A. (ed.), *The English Catholics, 1850–1950* (London, 1950), pp. 291–321. In a recent article on the failure of the Oxford Movement to fulfill its brilliant promise for English Catholicism, Ronald Chapman remarked, "On the one hand there is the enormous growth of the Church, and on the other its almost complete lack of influence. At the end of the century the Church is as much or more the Church of a minority than it was in the '50s."—"The Optimism of the 1840s," *The Tablet* (London), December 18, 1954.

hierarchy and coreligionists in the series of *Katholikentagen* to start a Catholic university were either frustrated by the hostility of the state or by the timidity and coolness of the Church's leaders. One has only to scan the pages of the quarterly *Hochland,* founded by Karl Muth over fifty years ago, to understand how little there was by way of a co-ordinated intellectual life among the German Catholics of the late nineteenth and early twentieth centuries. In fact, the editors of *Hochland* more than once drew down the frowns of ecclesiastical superiors for their attempts to establish a rapport with scholars outside the Church and to escape from the ghetto to which they felt the German Catholics had too long been confined. Yet in Germany there was a compensating factor that should not be overlooked, namely, that the absence of Catholic universities, and the state's requirements that degrees be earned in its own universities, brought Catholic professors—including the theologians—into the faculties of these universities where a number of them exercised national influence by their scholarship. This was the case with the famous Johann Görres of a century ago, and in our own day Martin Grabmann and Romano Guardini, to mention only two, have shown how helpful influence of this kind can be to the Church's standing in non-Catholic circles.[33]

---

[33]On the discontent current among a number of the German Catholic intellectuals of the late nineteenth and early twentieth centuries cf., for example, the speech of Georg von Hertling, a noted professor of philosophy in the University of Munich, and later Chancellor of Germany (October, 1917–September, 1918) to the general assembly of the Görres-Gesellschaft at Constance in September, 1896. On that occasion he pleaded with his fellow Catholics to take a more active part in serious scholarship rather than to confine themselves to works of apologetics for, as he said, "what we now need, are not so much the apologists as the true specialists, those who have tried with the armament of modern research to extend and to strengthen the sphere of human knowledge."—*Jahresbericht der Görres-Gesellschaft für das Jahr 1896* (Köln, 1896), pp. 16–23. Cf. also von Hertling's *Erinnerungen aus*

Moreover, the failure of American churchmen to find guidance and inspiration from a strong intellectual tradition in the lands of their ancestors was in no way compensated by the training they received in preparation for their priesthood, whether that be in diocesan seminaries or in the scholasticates of the religious orders. As Bishop Spalding stated at the Third Plenary Council of Baltimore: ". . . the ecclesiastical seminary is not a school of intellectual culture, either here in America or elsewhere, and to imagine that it can become the instrument of intellectual culture is to cherish a delusion. . . ."[34] Spalding rightly maintained that the seminary was, and must necessarily be, a training school for a profession, albeit a profession that might be expected to have more than an ordinary kinship for intellectual pursuits. But I wonder very much if the seminaries and scholasticates of our religious orders have made the most of their opportunities for intellectual stimulation and the cultivation of serious reading habits in their students that they should have. Speaking of the failure of the American priest to be more intellectually alive, John Talbot Smith, a respected New York

meinem Leben (München, 1920), II, 167–168. Over thirty years later Karl Muth lamented the timidity and narrow-mindedness of many of the Church's leaders when he asked, "Is it not a symptom of inner weakness, that Catholics and even the distinguished among them, priests included, have to turn to the non-Catholic press, if they wish to express an opinion differing from the official position? Where life is, there are antitheses and tensions. Harmony and lack of tension mean death."— "Pressa und 'Presse-not' Grundsätzliche Gedanken," *Hochland*, XXVI, Band I (November, 1928), 303. For further instances of this point of view cf. Matthias Laros, "Franz Xaver Kraus," *Hochland*, XXXVIII, Band I (October, 1940), 9–21 and "Wir deutschen Katholiken," *Kölnische Volkszeitung*, January 28, 1909. The author of the latter called for an examination of conscience on the part of the German Catholics which, he said, demanded not a "nervous, anxious narrowmindedness [and] shallow heresy-hunting, but a broadminded victory—confident tolerance in the thinking, striving, and acting of German Catholics."

[34]Spalding, *op.cit.*, p. 212.

priest, said nearly sixty years ago something which prompts one to ask if it is not still substantially true. He wrote:

> The habits of the intellectual life in the seminary have dwarfed him. The curriculum rarely recognizes anything but theology and philosophy, and these often isolated from present conditions and without practical knowledge. . . . [and] . . . . History is taught in random, unscientific fashion, to judge the method by the results. . . . It is not then a cause for wonder that the young priest should graduate so rude and unfinished. The wonder is that he should at all be able to hold his own in the sneering world, so skilled in knowledge of its times, so devoted to science and history. . . .[35]

Smith placed a good deal of responsibility on the hierarchy for the low state of intellectual endeavor among the priests of his generation, maintaining that to bring the entire educational system of the Church up to the mark was, as he said, "clearly the work of the episcopate, and no other power with which the church in America is acquainted can do that work."[36] Furthermore, he made it quite clear that he had in mind the religious orders as well as the diocesan priests, for with the religious superiors, too, he felt that only the bishops could bring about a change.

It may well be that Father Smith placed too heavy a burden of blame on the bishops of his day for the failure to foster a higher intellectual life among the clergy. But that their example and influence in these matters can exert a powerful influence in the lives of their subjects is beyond question. I happen to have been born in the Diocese of Peoria, and I knew at first hand the imprint left by Bishop John Lancaster Spalding on the intellectual tastes, the good reading, and the careful preparation of sermons of many of his priests. It was a subject for comment when I was growing up,

---

[35]John Talbot Smith, *Our Seminaries. An Essay on Clerical Training* (New York, 1896), p. 251.

[36]*Ibid.*, p. 253.

and I could personally verify from an acquaintance with several of these venerable priests the effect that these intellectual habits had upon their lives.

Nor am I aware of any noticeable difference between the American diocesan and religious order priests in this regard. Would it not be reasonable to expect that in religious orders, whose aims and energies are devoted in good measure to school work, that intellectual distinction would be fairly common? Yet if one bases a judgment on one of the most widely accepted criteria, namely, the production of scholarly books and learned reviews, the general record of the American religious has not been outstanding, nor would it profit by comparison with the achievements of their European confreres. Two of our most scholarly journals of clerical editorship were the *American Catholic Quarterly Review,* begun in January, 1876, and lasting to 1924, and the *American Ecclesiastical Review* which first appeared in January, 1889. To both of these periodicals members of the religious orders, to be sure, made valuable contributions through the years, but both owed their origin to secular priests, James A. Corcoran and Herman J. Heuser, who were professors in St. Charles Borromeo Seminary in Philadelphia. Another journal, one of the most learned the American Church ever knew, the *New York Review,* was the product of three professors of St. Joseph's Seminary in New York. It had been running only three years when the modernist scare frightened it out of existence in July, 1908. It was not until February, 1940, that the Jesuits began the publication of their quarterly, *Theological Studies,* of which every American Catholic intellectual is proud, and which can hold its head high in the company of the best European journals of its kind. Finally, the greatest single monument to Catholic scholarship in the United States to date has undoubtedly been the *Catholic Encyclopedia,* and that magnificent achievement owed its existence—as it should have—to the combined efforts of a small group of learned laymen and priests, both secular and regular.

No fair-minded man will underestimate the energies, the resources, and the thought which the clerical leaders of the Church in the United States have expended in behalf of education since the tiny Georgetown Academy first opened its doors to students in September, 1791. Moreover, the generosity—often at the price of genuine sacrifice—which the laity have shown in support of the Church's primary, secondary, collegiate, and seminary institutions has won the admiration of the Catholic world. Yet when one thinks in terms of the media through which distinction is normally won in the realm of advanced scholarship, namely, ample endowments for research, generous grants-in-aid to individual scholars, provision for extended leaves of absence from teaching duties, and the moral encouragement that comes from a consciousness that the Church's leaders are vitally interested and will effectively uphold the position of the Catholic intellectual, there has not been in our history the understanding or appreciation of the problems involved that there should have been. Perhaps I can best illustrate what I mean by an example. In 1951 Father Philip Hughes published the first of his superb three-volume work, *The Reformation in England* (New York, 1951–1954). And these volumes, it should be remarked, are only the latest among approximately a dozen solid publications which Father Hughes has written—and that on his own with little or no financial assistance—since he took his degree at the Catholic University of Louvain in 1921. Several months after Volume I appeared the *Oxford Magazine* carried a review which opened with this sentence, "This is one of the rare books which it is almost an impertinence to praise." After two pages of the highest commendation the review closed as follows: "If England is ever to be re-won to the papal allegiance, if a parlous Christendom is ever to be inspired to close its ranks, it will be by honest writing of this kind."[37] That kind of review of a work by a Catholic historian on his own

---

[37]A. O. in *Oxford Magazine,* LXIX (February 1, 1951), 242–244.

Church, coming out of Oxford is, I submit, worth more than money can buy to Catholic scholarship. Yet when the American Catholic Historical Association in December, 1954, conferred on Father Hughes its John Gilmary Shea Prize for his three volumes on the Protestant Revolt in England, he told me in a letter, "It is the first recognition I have ever had, and it is from my own. It touches me too deeply for me to find words to say all I feel about it."[38] How many American Catholic scholars, both living and dead, could tell a similar tale of the failure of their own to recognize their scholarly accomplishments and to lend them their support?

Part of the reason why American Catholics have not made a notable impression on the intellectual life of their country is due, I am convinced, to what might be called a betrayal of that which is peculiarly their own. The nature of that betrayal has been high-lighted during the last quarter of a century by such movements as the scholastic revival in philosophy which found its most enthusiastic and hard-working friends on the campuses of the University of Chicago, the University of Virginia, Princeton University, and St. John's College, Annapolis. Meanwhile the Catholic universities were engrossed in their mad pursuit of every passing fancy that crossed the American educational scene, and found relatively little time for distinguished contributions to scholastic philosophy. Woefully lacking in the endowment, training, and equipment to make them successful competitors of the secular universities in fields like engineering, business administration, nursing education, and the like, the Catholic universities, nonetheless, went on multiplying these units and spreading their budgets so thin—in an attempt to include everything—that the subjects in which they could, and should, make a unique contribution were sorely neglected.

That American educators expect Catholic institutions to be strong in the humanities and the liberal arts—to say nothing of

---

[38]Philip Hughes to the writer, London, December 14, 1954.

theology and philosophy—is not surprising. Eighteen years ago
Robert M. Hutchins, then President of the University of Chicago,
in an address before the Middle West regional unit of the National
Catholic Educational Association made that point in a very forceful way. Speaking of the Catholic Church as having what he called
"the longest intellectual tradition of any institution in the contemporary world," Hutchins criticized the Catholic institutions for
failing to emphasize that tradition in a way that would make it come
alive in American intellectual circles. He thought the ideals of
Catholic educators were satisfactory, but as far as actual practice
was concerned, he said, "I find it necessary to level against you a
scandalous accusation." He then went on:

> In my opinion . . . you have imitated the worst features
> of secular education and ignored most of the good ones. There
> are some good ones, relatively speaking—high academic
> standards, development of habits of work, and research. . . .[39]

Hutchins listed the bad features he had in mind as athleticism, col-
legiatism, vocationalism, and anti-intellectualism. In regard to the
first two we can claim, I think, that in recent years Catholic institutions have shown improvement, just as all other educational groups
have done. As for the second two, vocationalism and anti-intellectualism, I find no striking evidence of reform in the Church's
colleges and universities since 1937. Regarding the three good features of secular institutions which Hutchins named, high academic
standards, development of habits of work, and the ideal of research,
I would say that a better showing has been made here and there on
the first, but in the development of habits of work and a cherished
ideal of research, I cannot personally see much by way of a fundamental change.

---

[39]Robert M. Hutchins, "The Integrating Principle of Catholic Higher
Education," *College Newsletter, Midwest Regional Unit, N.C.E.A.*
(May, 1937), p. 1.

A second major defect in Catholic higher education that helps to account for its paucity of scholars of distinction, is what I would call our betrayal of one another. By that I mean the development within the last two decades of numerous and competing graduate schools, none of which is adequately endowed, and few of which have the trained personnel, the equipment in libraries and laboratories, and the professional wage scales to warrant their ambitious undertakings. The result is a perpetuation of mediocrity and the draining away from each other of the strength that is necessary if really superior achievements are to be attained. I am speaking here, incidentally, only of the graduate schools, and not of the competition—amounting in certain places to internecine warfare—among the more than 200 Catholic colleges of the land. In both categories, however, the situation is serious, and if Benjamin Fine, writing in the New York *Times* of May 8, 1955, is to be believed, there is every prospect that it will become more serious. There is, and there has been for years, a desperate need for some kind of planning for Catholic higher education on a national scale. As to the likelihood of such in the immediate future, there would seem to be little room for optimism. One might, perhaps, illustrate the point by a parallel in international relations.

When the French National Assembly voted down the European Defense Community in August, 1954, a shudder went through the free world. Every man of perception realized that if the historic rivals of western Europe did not lay aside their differences there was a real chance that one by one they would perish at the hands of Russia and its satellites. Nothing less than that drastic alternative wrought a change of heart during the ensuing months, and it was the deep-seated fear of that grim fate that brought the representatives of the seven nations to Paris on May 7, 1955, to set their signatures to the newly formed Council of the Western European Union. The Catholic institutions of higher learning in this country may soon face an equally grave threat to their survival. It will not be the peril of communist occupation that will bring them together to counsel for their mutual welfare, but it may well be a thing that Americans understand much better, namely, the peril of financial bankruptcy. I realize that this may sound extreme, but in my judgment the danger of insolvency, and that alone, will put an end to the senseless duplication of effort and the wasteful proliferation that have robbed Catholic graduate schools of the hope of superior achievement in the restricted area of those academic disciplines where their true strength and mission lie. Hutchins had that in mind when he closed his address to the Catholic educators at Chicago in 1937 by saying, "The best service Catholic education can perform for the nation and all education is to show that the intellectual tradition can again be made the heart of higher education."[40]

An additional point which should find place in an investigation of this kind is the absence of a love of scholarship for its own sake among American Catholics, and that even among too large a number of Catholics who are engaged in higher education. It might be described as the absence of a sense of dedication to an intellectual apostolate. This defect, in turn, tends to deprive many of those who spend their lives in the universities of the American Church of the admirable industry and unremitting labor in research and publication which characterize a far greater proportion of their colleagues on the faculties of the secular universities. I do not pretend to know precisely what the cause of this may be, but I wonder if it is not in part due to the too literal interpretation which many churchmen and superiors of seminaries and religious houses have given to St. Paul's oft-quoted statement that "Here we have no permanent city, but we seek for the city that is to come,"[41] and their emphasis on the question of the author of the *Imitation of Christ*

---

[40]*Ibid.*, p. 4.

[41]Hebrews, 13: 14.

when he asked, "What doth it avail thee to discourse profoundly of the Trinity, if thou be void of humility, and consequently displeasing to the Trinity?"[42] Too frequently, perhaps, those training in our institutions have had the same author's famous dictum, "I had rather feel compunction than know its definition," quoted to them without a counterbalancing emphasis on the evils of intellectual sloth. Certainly no intellectual who is worthy of the name Catholic would deny the fundamental importance of humility as an indispensable virtue in the life of the follower of Christ. But the danger of intellectual pride, grave as it is, should not be allowed to obscure the lesson taught by our Lord in the parable of the talents. If that principle had been pressed too far by Albertus Magnus we might never have known the *Summa theologiae* of St. Thomas Aquinas. Many may still recall a less dignified example of this mistaken emphasis when William Jennings Bryan gave eminent satisfaction to a Baptist fundamentalist audience in New York in 1923 with his declaration: "If we have come to the stage at which we must decide between geology and Christianity, I think it is better to know the Rock of Ages than the age of rocks."[43]

Closely connected with the question of the prevailing Catholic attitudes in education is the overemphasis which some authorities of the Church's educational system in the United States have given to the school as an agency for moral development, with an insufficient stress on the role of the school as an instrument for fostering intellectual excellence. That fact has at times led to a confusion of aims and to a neglect of the school as a training ground for the intellectual virtues. No sensible person will for a moment question that the inculcation of moral virtue is one of the principal reasons for having Catholic schools in any circumstances. But that goal

---

[42]Thomas à Kempis, *The Imitation of Christ* (Baltimore, n.d.), p. 2.
[43]New York *Times,* December 8, 1923.

should never be permitted to overshadow the fact that the school, at whatever level one may consider it, must maintain a strong emphasis on the cultivation of intellectual excellence. Given superior minds, out of the striving for the intellectual virtues there will flow, with its attendant religious instruction, the formation of a type of student who will not only be able to withstand the strains which life will inevitably force upon his religious faith, but one who will have been so intellectually fortified that he will reflect distinction upon the system of which he is a product.[44]

Up to this point I have assumed general agreement as to the impoverishment of Catholic scholarship in this country, as well as to the low state of Catholic leadership in most walks of national life. The assumption has, I believe, been a safe one even though there has not been advanced any documentary coverage of the case. Let us now examine briefly the picture that has emerged from a few of the many studies that have been made in the last quarter century on the subject of the relationship between religious affiliation and national leadership, especially in intellectual affairs.

In the summer of 1927 the *American Mercury* carried an article on the relation of religious affiliation to the names selected for *Who's Who in America*. In this instance it was found that only seven out of every 100,000 Catholic men were listed in that directory, compared to a ratio of eleven per 100,000 among the Seventh Day Adventists and twenty per 100,000 among the Jews.[45] In the same year William S. Ament of Scripps College made an analysis of 1,013 names in *Who's Who in America*. Among those whose religion was given he discovered that there were 224 Episcopalians, 208 Presbyterians, sixty-one Unitarians, but only thirty-eight Cath-

---

[44]On this point cf. Edward J. Power, "Orestes A. Brownson on Catholic Schools," *Homiletic and Pastoral Review*, LV (April, 1955), 568.

[45]Ellsworth Huntington and Leo F. Whitney, "Religion and 'Who's Who,'" *American Mercury*, XI (August, 1927), 440.

olics, with the Episcopalians representing 22.2 per cent of the total and the Catholics 3.8 per cent. The distribution of the thirty-eight Catholics showed: eleven bishops and priests; eight in arts and letters; seven in law and public service; six in business; four in school administration and teaching; and two in science.[46] A third study of this kind in the *Scientific Monthly* of December, 1931, gathered its data mainly from the standard guide, *American Men of Science,* with a view to determining the relationship between scientific eminence and church membership. Out of a total of 303 top scientists investigated only three were Catholics, which prompted the quite unfounded conclusion that "The conspicuous dearth of scientists among the Catholics suggests that the tenets of that church are not consonant with scientific endeavor."[47]

Of far more significance, however, than this study of 1931 in judging the status of Catholic scientists in the United States is a volume published three years ago by R. H. Knapp and H. B. Goodrich. These investigators sifted 18,000 names from among the 43,500 scientists listed in two editions of *American Men of Science.* From these selected names they then drew up a list of the fifty institutions which had led in the production of scientists, but no Catholic college or university received a place among the fifty leaders. Knapp and Goodrich remark: "A closer examination of the Catholic institutions reveals that, without exception, they lie

---

[46]William S. Ament, "Religion, Education and Distinction," *School and Society,* XXVI (September 24, 1927), 403.

[47]Harvey C. Lehman and Paul A. Witty, "Scientific Eminence and Church Membership," *Scientific Monthly,* XXXIII (December, 1931), 549. Stephen Sargent Visher, *Scientists Starred, 1903–1943 in "American Men of Science"* (Baltimore, 1947), embodied the results of the Lehman-Witty study in his volume, where he showed that of the fourteen denominations examined the Congregationalists were first with sixty-six scientists starred, or 21.8 per cent of the total, while the Catholics were the next to last with three or 1.0 per cent of the whole (pp. 535–536).

among the least productive 10 per cent of all institutions and constitute a singularly unproductive sample."[48] Reed College headed
the list for the entire country during both periods surveyed. In the
years 1924–1934 it produced 132 scientists per 1,000 male graduates, while for the years 1930–1941 it again led with ninety-eight
per 1,000 male graduates. By comparison the Catholic liberal arts
colleges produced only 2.8 scientists per 1,000 male graduates and
the Catholic universities only 1.7 per 1,000 male graduates. Insofar as the authors were able to ascertain such factors as financial
resources, student-faculty ratio, cost of attendance, and the quality
of students differed but little in Catholic institutions from the general run of American colleges and universities.[49] It is a conclusion

---

[48]R. H. Knapp and H. B. Goodrich, *Origins of American Scientists*
(Chicago, 1952), p. 24.

[49]*Ibid.,* p. 288. It is evident that Knapp and Goodrich were at something of a loss to account for the conspicuous and uniformly low standing of Catholic institutions in their survey. In an effort to explain it they
listed four possible causes: (a) Catholic institutions are in good part
concentrated in the eastern industrial part of the country, "a region not
noted for high production of scientists"; (b) Catholics have been drawn
from European stocks which in recent times have not been outstanding
in scientific achievement; (c) the Church permits comparatively little
secularization of attiude on the part of its faithful and maintains a "firm
authoritarian structure"; (d) the Church has been a consistent opponent
of philosophical monism, "that philosophic tradition under which
science has for the most part advanced" (*ibid.*). Another index to this
situation is afforded by the awards of the National Science Foundation.
In the awards announced for the year 1955–1956, only 4.6 per cent of
the 151 awards in physics went to Catholics and 1.2 per cent of the
167 awards granted in chemistry. Of the first-year awards, which relate
more directly to the situation prevailing in Catholic undergraduate colleges, about 4.5 per cent were made to Catholics. In the "honorable mention" category the Catholic showing was somewhat better with eighty-
eight out of a total of 1,409. The University of Notre Dame was far
ahead of all other Catholic institutions in these awards with Notre
Dame, the Catholic University of America, and Manhattan College ac-
counting for nearly one-half of the total. Incidentally, half of the life

with which—save for the point of financial resources—I think most Catholic educators would be inclined to agree.

A different approach to the problem of distinction among the Catholic scientists of this country was afforded when Pope Pius XI reconstituted the Pontifical Academy of Sciences in October, 1936. Out of seventy names chosen at that time six were from the United States, but only one, George S. Sperti of the Institutum Divi Thomae of Cincinnati, was connected with a Catholic institution. It is worthy of note, I think, that of these seventy scientists selected by the Holy See five were members of the faculty of the Catholic University of Louvain. According to the *Annuario pontificio* for 1954 there were then seven Americans in the academy, but only two, Sperti and Edward A. Doisy of Saint Louis University, were from Catholic institutions.[50] And when Pope Pius XII some months ago announced fourteen new appointments the only one of these teaching in an American institution was Theodore von Karman, a Hungarian-born non-Catholic who is Director of the Guggenheim Laboratory at the California Institute of Technology.[51]

If the Catholic scientists should have begun to think that an undue amount of stress has been placed on the dearth of distinguished names among their kind, they can be quickly reassured. The picture in the sacred sciences, the liberal arts, and the humanities is no brighter on that score, for the studies which I have examined reveal no higher proportion of distinction in these fields than they do in science. Nearly thirty years ago George N. Shuster, whose principal interest lies in literature, went over this ground

---

science citations among Catholics went to students in the Catholic women's colleges. James J. Huddick, S.J., "The National Science Foundation Awards for 1955–1956," *Bulletin of the Albertus Magnus Guild*, II (May, 1955), 5–6.

[50] *Annuario pontificio per l'anno 1954* (Città del Vaticano, 1954), pp. 1035–1038.

[51] New York *Times*, April 17, 1955.

and reached the same conclusion about the facts of the situation that most of us hold today.[52] In 1939 John A. O'Brien edited a symposium, embracing all fields, which produced an equally bleak picture,[53] and two years later when Theodore Maynard, with special emphasis on literature and the arts, devoted a lengthy chapter to a survey of the Catholic cultural contribution to the United States, he arrived at an ending that was not much happier than that of his predecessors.[54]

Most of these men made passing mention of the relatively high proportion of scholarly contributions that had marked the careers of many of the converts to the Church during the present century. But no one of them brought that fact home with the force of a book which appeared in 1944 from a brother of the Congregation of Holy Cross.[55] As one studies the 259 biographical sketches in Brother David's volume, extending in time from 1783 when John Thayer, the Congregationalist minister of Boston, was converted

---

[52]George N. Shuster, *The Catholic Spirit in America* (New York, 1927), pp. 163–204.

[53]John A. O'Brien (ed.), *Catholics and Scholarship* (Huntington, 1939).

[54]Theodore Maynard, *The Story of American Catholicism* (New York, 1941), pp. 543–586. For a highly critical view of the failure of American Catholics to create a distinguished literature cf. Harry Sylvester, "Problems of the Catholic Writer," *Atlantic Monthly,* CLXXXI (January, 1948), 109–113. On the low fortunes of the American Catholic press cf. Neil MacNeil, "The Needs of the Catholic Press," *America,* LXXVIII (February 21, 1938), 574–575.

[55]David [Martin], C.S.C., *American Catholic Convert Authors. A Bio-Bibliography* (Detroit, 1944). The research of my seminar student, Mother Mary Peter Carthy, O.S.U., on the productive scholarship of lay Catholics in the 1940's bears out the conclusion concerning the proportionately high number of converts among those who have had distinguished publications. An analysis of Catholic scholars in the United States from the viewpoint of foreign birth and training would, I suspect, prove equally revealing.

to 1942 when Helene Magaret was received into the Church, one wonders where the intellectual life of the Church of the United States would have been without them. Needless to say, every Catholic is grateful that so many converts of scholarly tastes and habits have found the grace of conversion and have put their talents at the disposal of the American Church. But it does raise the disquieting thought of how much more dismal the intellectual record would have been were it to have depended solely on those who were Catholics from birth. In the case of practically all of these convert scholars Catholic education can take no credit whatever, for they were what they were and are, intellectually speaking, when the grace of the Holy Spirit illumined their minds and led them to find a lasting place amongst us. This has been strikingly true in history, for the scholarly accomplishments of the American convert historians of the twentieth century have been altogether conspicuous. To mention only one, when the American Historical Association, for the first and only time in its seventy years of life, bestowed its presidency on a Catholic in 1945 it was Carlton J. H. Hayes who was chosen. And no one requires enlightenment about the luster shed upon the Catholic body of this country for over half a century by the notable contributions to the history of modern Europe of that honored name.

More recent studies have, moreover, borne out the findings of earlier writers on the lack of distinction among Catholics in fields like the humanities and liberal arts. For example, in 1941 B. W. Kunkel of Lafayette College classified 54,076 graduate students representing colleges whose undergraduate enrollment totaled 360,-317. Among the thirty-six colleges which had furnished at least 12 per cent of their total enrollment to graduate schools proper, no Catholic school was represented.[56] However, in the number of their

---

[56]B. W. Kunkel, "The Representation of Colleges in Graduate and Professional Schools in the United States," *Association of American*

graduates who entered schools of law and medicine the Catholic colleges made a much better showing. In the forty-eight law schools that responded to the inquiry there were found to be twenty-eight institutions that had at least 3.6 per cent of their total enrollment in these law schools. Here Georgetown University led the list with 21.2 per cent, Harvard being second with 12.8 per cent, while Holy Cross, Fordham, Notre Dame, and Manhattan appeared among the twenty-eight in that order. Of thirty-five colleges with 5 per cent or more of their alumni enrolled in the fifty-two medical schools studied by Kunkel, Villanova University was in tenth place with 9.0 per cent, while St. Peter's, Holy Cross, and Creighton also showed among the thirty-five leaders in this category.[57] But among those schools that had furnished the highest per cent of their liberal arts and engineering alumni to graduate and professional schools

---

Colleges Bulletin, XXVII (October, 1941), 457. In weighing Kunkel's over-all figures, however, allowance must be made for the fact that they include no data for the students who entered Catholic seminaries after graduation from college, although theological schools constituted one of the four kinds of graduate and professional schools examined in this survey. The author is careful to call attention several times to this omission (pp. 451, 455, 456, 462). But nowhere is it made clear whether he did not seek the pertinent data from the Catholic seminaries, or whether he sought it and it was not forthcoming. The closest approach to the point suggests that Kunkel tried to get the figures and failed. Speaking of Fordham University's over-all figure he says, "it does not include theological students of Fordham's alumni since no information was received from the Catholic seminaries" (p. 462). If this is a correct interpretation of the author's remark it is regrettable that the authorities of the seminaries approached failed to respond to the questionnaire.

[57]*Ibid.,* p. 456. Knapp & Goodrich noted the relatively high number of graduates of Catholic colleges who go on for law, which led them to remark, "So far as we can judge, it appears that the Catholic institutions as a group are dedicated to training primarily in nonscientific fields. Indeed, Kunkel's study . . . suggests that the production of lawyers from Catholic institutions is as phenomenally high as their production of scientists is low" (*op. cit.,* p. 51).

collectively—Temple University was in the lead with 49.8 per cent and Randolph-Macon was last with 20 per cent—no Catholic school received mention. It would seem evident, therefore, that in the period covered by Kunkel's investigation Catholic colleges produced a better than average number of students for schools of law and medicine, but a relatively small number who continued their training in graduate schools properly so called.

While it is gratifying to learn that so many of the graduates of Catholic institutions pursue their studies beyond college by fitting themselves for the legal and medical professions, it is to be regretted that a proportionately high number do not manifest a like desire, or find a similarly strong stimulation, to become trained scholars in the fields where the Catholic tradition of learning is the strongest. In that connection the work of Robert H. Knapp and Joseph J. Greenbaum published two years ago is enlightening. The principal objective of these authors was to determine, from the undergraduate backgrounds of the younger generation of Americans who had won distinction in graduate schools during the years 1946–1952, which colleges had produced the largest number of promising scholars. A poll of some 7,000 individuals was taken according to the following norms: (a) earned a Ph.D. since 1948 in one of twenty-five universities sampled; (b) won a university fellowship or scholarship since 1946 from one of these twenty-five universities; (c) received a private fellowship since 1946 from one of nine private foundations sampled; (d) awarded a government fellowship since 1946 from one of three agencies, namely, Public Health Service, Atomic Energy Commission, and United States Department of State under the Fulbright Program.[58]

The roster assembled by Knapp and Greenbaum contained in all the names of 562 institutions, but among the fifty top-ranking

---

[58]Robert H. Knapp and Joseph J. Greenbaum, *The Younger American Scholar: His Collegiate Origins* (Chicago, 1953), p. 8.

colleges for men in the production of scholars in science, social science, and the humanities, no Catholic school found a place.[59] From among the total number of institutions the authors selected 138 colleges to constitute what they termed the "Liberal Arts Sample." These institutions were chosen by reason of the fact that they were free from vocationalism, privately controlled, committed to general education, and were without full programs of graduate study. On the basis of institutional control a threefold division was made according to whether the college was under nondenominational, Protestant, or Catholic auspices. In the realm of the humanities it was found that 38.7 per cent had come from Protestant colleges, 23.4 per cent from the nondenominational schools, but only 8.3 per cent from the Catholic institutions. The poor showing of Catholics in the humanities was a source of surprise to Knapp and Greenbaum. Speaking of their false assumption that the South was weak in science, they said:

> Similarly, we had expected that Catholic institutions would be marked by relatively large contributions to the field of humanities. In this speculation, however, we were again mistaken. Catholic institutions, though exceptionally unproductive in all areas of scholarship, achieve their best record in the sciences.[60]

Although these authors more than once protest the partial nature of the evidence upon which their findings were based and warn against drawing hard and fast conclusions from their limited data, it is, nonetheless, significant that they should have been brought to the conclusion that in every one of the categories of their investigation—distinction won in science, social science, and the humanities, earning a Ph.D., and winning an award from government, univer-

---

[59]*Ibid.*, p. 16.

[60]*Ibid.*, p. 99.

sity, or private foundation—"the Catholic institutions are consistently the lowest of all seven partial indices."[61]

The one bright spot of the Knapp-Greenbaum study, insofar as Catholics are concerned, relates to the women's colleges. In a chapter on "The Origins of Female Scholars of Distinction," twelve schools that led in the production of scholars were named with Bryn Mawr heading the list and Siena Heights College, Adrian, Michigan, in tenth place.[62] Among the fourteen women's colleges with less than 400 graduates in the years 1946–1952, constituting what was called the "Small Sample," Nazareth College, Nazareth, Michigan, led the list with five awards out of 135 graduates, Swarthmore was second with thirteen awards out of 397 graduates, Aquinas College, Grand Rapids, was sixth with three awards out of 170 graduates, and Loretto Heights College, Denver, was in twelfth place with three awards out of 282 graduates.[63] These facts would tend to bear out a fairly common opinion that in a number of ways the Catholic women's colleges are in advance of the institutions for men. The over-all impression left by the Knapp-Greenbaum work is, therefore, anything but flattering to the Catholic institutions of this country, especially in fields like the humanities and the social sciences.

In conclusion, then, one may say that it has been a combination of all the major points made in this paper, along with others which I may have failed to consider, that has produced in American Catholics generally, as well as in the intellectuals, a pervading spirit of separatism from their fellow citizens of other religious faiths. They have suffered from the timidity that characterizes minority groups, from the effects of a ghetto they have themselves fostered,

---

[61]*Ibid.*, p. 45.

[62]*Ibid.*, p. 70.

[63]*Ibid.*, p. 73.

and, too, from a sense of inferiority induced by their consciousness
of the inadequacy of Catholic scholarship. But who, one may
rightly ask, has been responsible in the main for its inadequacy?
Certainly not the Church's enemies, for if one were to reason on
that basis St. Augustine would never have written the *City of God,*
St. Robert Bellarmine the *Tractatus de potestate summi pontificis,*
nor would Cardinal Baronius have produced the *Annales ecclesias-
tici.* In fact, it has been enmity and opposition that have called
forth some of the greatest monuments to Catholic scholarship. The
major defect, therefore, lies elsewhere than with the unfriendly
attitude of some of those outside the Church. The chief blame, I
firmly believe, lies with Catholics themselves. It lies in their frequently self-imposed ghetto mentality which prevents them from
mingling as they should with their non-Catholic colleagues, and in
their lack of industry and the habits of work, to which Hutchins
alluded in 1937. It lies in their failure to have measured up to
their responsibilities to the incomparable tradition of Catholic learning of which they are the direct heirs, a failure which Peter Viereck
noted, and which suggested to him the caustic question, "Is the
honorable adjective 'Roman Catholic' truly merited by America's
middleclass-Jansenist Catholicism, puritanized, Calvinized, and de-
hydrated . . .?"[64] When the inescapable and exacting labor of true

---

[64] Peter Viereck, *Shame and Glory of the Intellectuals* (Boston, 1953),
p. 49. Speaking of the fact that the contemporary world crisis has been
caused by a process of continuous secularization of what was origi-
nally produced and developed under Christian auspices, Heinrich Rommen has said, "It is for this reason that Catholics cannot simply sur-
render what in a twofold sense is theirs as Catholics and as men, but
must irradiate their faith, informed by charity, into their own beleaguered democracy; a flight into a Catholic ghetto, into a catacombs,
is a kind of treason today."—"Catholicism and American Democracy,"
Catholicism in American Culture (New Rochelle, 1955), p. 68. Professor Rommen's essay was one of five lectures delivered at the College of
New Rochelle during the academic year 1953–1954 to mark the golden
jubilee of the college.

scholarship is intelligently directed and competently expressed it will win its way on its own merits into channels of influence beyond the Catholic pale. Of that one can be certain. For example, during the last year thousands of Americans have been brought into contact with the thought and research of two Catholic scholars, Francis G. Wilson and John Courtney Murray, S.J., on vital aspects of the current crisis through the use that has been made of them by Walter Lippmann in his latest book.[65]

Yet an effective result of this kind is only attained through unremitting labor, prolonged thought, and a sense of the exalted mission of the intellectual apostolate on the part of the Catholic scholar. It was that ideal that Newman kept before him during his famous lectures on the position of the English Catholics at the Birmingham Oratory in the summer of 1851. He challenged his hearers to be equal to the obligation they owed to their non-Catholic fellow-countrymen. As he said:

> They must be made to know us as we are; they must be made to know our religion as it is, not as they fancy it; they must be made to look at us, and they are overcome. This is the work that lies before you in your place and in your measure.[66]

There is not a man of discernment anywhere today who is unaware that the intellectual climate of the United States is undergoing a radical change from the moribund philosophy of materialism and discredited liberalism that have ruled a good portion of the American mind for the better part of a century. Clinton Rossiter spoke of this in a thoughtful article published some months ago. He fore-

---

[65]Walter Lippmann, *The Public Philosophy* (New York, 1955), pp. 96, 177–178. Other Catholic authors cited by Lippmann are Thomas J. Slater, S.J., Etienne Gilson, and Yves Simon; cf. pp. 48, 85, 110, and 148.

[66]John Henry Newman, *Lectures on the Present Position of the Catholics in England* (New York, 1913), p. 378.

sees a new day dawning for our country when religious and moral values will again be found in the honored place they once occupied. Concerning that ray of hope upon the horizon, he concluded: "And it will rest its own strong faith in liberty and constitutional democracy on the bedrock of these traditional, indeed eternal values: religion, justice, morality."[67] If this prediction should prove true, and there is increasing support for the view that it will, to whom, one may ask, may the leaders of the coming generation turn with more rightful expectancy in their search for enlightenment and guidance in the realm of religion and morality than to the American Catholic intellectuals? For it is they who are in possession of the oldest, wisest, and most sublime tradition of learning that the world has ever known. There has, indeed, been considerable improvement among American Catholics in the realm of intellectual affairs in the last half-century, but the need for far more energetic strides is urgent if the receptive attitude of contemporary thought is to be capitalized upon as it should be. It is, therefore, a unique opportunity that lies before the Catholic scholars of the United States which, if approached and executed with the deep conviction of its vital importance for the future of the American Church, may inspire them to do great things and, at the end, to feel that they have in some small measure lived up to the ideal expressed by Père Sertillanges when he said of the Catholic intellectuals:

> They, more than others, must be men consecrated by their vocation. . . . The special asceticism and the heroic virtue of the intellectual worker must be their daily portion. But if they consent to this double self-offering, I tell them in the name of the God of Truth not to lose courage.[68]

---

[67]Clinton Rossiter, "Toward an American Conservatism," *Yale Review,* XLIV (Spring, 1955), 372.

[68]A. D. Sertillanges, O.P., *The Intellectual Life* (Westminster, Maryland, 1947), p. 16.

Index

61